WE ARE HERE

WE ARE HERE

NIELS HAV

TRANSLATED FROM THE DANISH BY
P.K. BRASK AND PATRICK FRIESEN

BookThug Toronto

LIBRARY AND ARCHIVES CANADA
CATALOGUING IN PUBLICATION

Hav, Niels, 1949-
　We are here / Niels Hav ; translated from the Danish by
Patrick Friesen and P.K. Brask.

Translaton of: Grundstof.
Poems.
ISBN 0-9781587-2-5
I. Friesen, Patrick, 1946- II. Brask, Per K., 1952- III. Title.

PT8176.18.A9G7813 2006　　　839.81'174　　C2006-905181-X

CONTENTS

A MYSTERY

The greatest mystery for the composer
who for 47 years has seriously explored sound

Is the catchy little song on the radio
every morning which everyone hums along with and whistles

On the way out to the car and sings in the street
at night when they are happy and just let go

That is a mystery!

I have once again fallen in love
this time with five different women during a ride
on the number 40 bus from Njalsgade to Østerbro.
How is one to gain control of one's life under such conditions?
One wore a fur coat, another red wellingtons.
One of them was reading a newspaper, the other Heidegger
– and the streets were flooded with rain.
At Amager Boulevard a drenched princess entered,
euphoric and furious, and I fell for her utterly.
But she jumped off at the police station
and was replaced by two queens with flaming kerchiefs,
who spoke shrilly with each other in Pakistani
all the way to the Municipal Hospital while the bus boiled
in poetry. They were sisters and equally beautiful,
so I lost my heart to both of them and immediately planned
a new life in a village near Rawalpindi
where children grow up in the scent of hibiscus
while their desperate mothers sing heartbreaking songs
as dusk settles over the Pakistani plains.

But they didn't see me!
And the one wearing a fur coat cried beneath
her glove when she got off at Farimagsgade.
The girl reading Heidegger suddenly shut her book
and looked directly at me with a dirisive smile,
as if she'd suddenly caught a glimpse of Mr. Nobody
in his very own insignificance.
And that's how my heart broke for the fifth time,
when she got up and left the bus with all the others.
                              Life is so brutal.
I continued for two more stops before giving up.
It always ends like that: You stand alone
on the kerb, sucking on a cigarette,
wound up and mildly unhappy.

Human mentality is a mystical hotel
with many floors, corridors, meeting rooms
and conference facilities.
At reception indisputable common sense rules
during the day. At night everything is taken care of
by a Neanderthal.

All world views are represented in this hotel.
In some rooms important contracts are negotiated,
drastic reforms are planned. Criminal
acts and murder are contemplated. If the receptionist
knocks on this door to ask personal questions
he will be turned away with a roar of derision.
In other rooms philosophers live, word jugglers,
shamans and zealous believers. The basement is haunted
by the great drummer of nothingness who keeps
reptiles as pets. Everywhere there's febrile activity.

In crucial situations everyone is called together
for a conference, night or day, in order to consult
on big problems or pure trivialities.
There's no agenda and no chair;
questions rise and disappear in quick riots.
One argument on top of another
each at its own pitch. Some use logic
or common sense, others declaim with howls,
whining, song, curses, pleas and screams of terror.
Ancient spirits chant reams of incomprehensible words
in dead languages. Rarely
is a binding conclusion drawn.
Suddenly everyone returns to their rooms
each snared in his own unshakeable confusion.

At reception a clean, well-dressed
person walks about. He calls himself I
and maintains that he's the manager; he asserts
that all decisions are made by him; he claims

that the hotel is rationally run
in accordance with contemporary principles.

Listen to him with a little skepticism.
The rest of the hotel's inhabitants don't give a penny
for his authority.

Some words are more beautiful than the experience they stand for,
for example the word illumination. In my mind I see Odense;
the poet standing in the open window at city hall
with tears in his eyes, torches outside in the dark,
the poet's emotion, the hearty hand shakes.
All of it a fulfillment of the old prophecy;
now the city is illuminated for him.
It is all genuine. The tears are real tears.
But the toothache is unbearable, the icy air
enflames the pain terribly:
Instead of properly enjoying the happiness
of these minutes that will never return,
I looked at the song sheet to see how many verses
remained before I could be rid of the torture
the cold air forced me to suffer through my teeth.

I prefer writing
with a used pen found in the street
or with a promotional pen, gladly one from the electricians,
the gas station or the bank.
Not just because they are cheap (free),
but I imagine that such an implement
will fuse my writing with industry
the sweat of skilled labourers, administrative offices
and the mystery of all existence.

Once I wrote meticulous poems with a fountain pen
– pure poetry about purely nothing –
but now I like shit on my paper
tears and snot.

Poetry is not for sissies.
A poem must be just as honest as the Dow Jones index
– a mixture of reality and sheer bluff.
What has one grown too sensitive for?
Not much.

That's why I keep my eye on the bond market
and serious pieces of paper. The stock exchange
belongs to reality – just like poetry.
And that's why I'm so happy about this ball point pen
from the bank, which I found one dark night
in front of a closed convenience store. It smells
faintly of dog piss, and it writes fantastically.

What are we to do about the poets?
Life's rough on them
they look so pitiful dressed in black
their skin blue from internal blizzards.

Poetry is a horrible disease
the infected walk about complaining
their screams pollute the atmosphere like leaks
from atomic power stations of the mind. It's so psychotic.
Poetry is a tyrant
it keeps people awake at night and destroys marriages
it draws people out to desolate cottages in mid-winter
where they sit in pain wearing earmuffs and thick scarves.
Imagine the torture.

Poetry is a pest
worse than gonorrhea, a terrible abomination.
But consider poets it's hard for them
bear with them.
They are hysterical as if they are expecting twins
they gnash their teeth while sleeping, they eat dirt
and grass. They stay out in the howling wind for hours
tormented by astounding metaphors.
Every day is a holy day for them.

Oh please, take pity on the poets
they are deaf and blind
help them through traffic where they stagger about
with their invisible handicap
remembering all sorts of stuff. Now and then one of them stops
to listen for a distant siren.
Show consideration for them.

Poets are like insane children
who've been chased from their homes by the entire family.
Pray for them
they are born unhappy

their mothers have cried for them
sought the assistance of doctors and lawyers, until they had to give up
for fear of losing their own minds.
Oh, cry for the poets.

Nothing can save them.
Infested with poetry like secret lepers
they are incarcerated in their own fantasy world
a gruesome ghetto filled with demons
and vindictive ghosts.

When on a clear summer's day the sun shining brightly
you see a poor poet
come wobbling out of the apartment block, looking pale
like a cadaver and disfigured by speculations
then walk up and help him.
Tie his shoelaces, lead him to the park
and help him sit down on the bench
in the sun. Sing to him a little
buy him an ice cream and tell him a story
because he's so sad.
He's completely ruined by poetry.

OFTEN IT'S BEEN A COMFORT

Often it's been a comfort
to think of Erik Knudsen
who toils up at Humlebæk.
Summer and winter;
he exists.

Once I spoke with him
on the phone. – I'm not a poet
he said, only
when I'm writing.

SILENCE

It's a mystery: as young people
we can exchange experiences, defeats
and victories in full appreciation.
We can talk our way toward each other;
all choices are still provisional
and without serious consequences.

Later that becomes impossible.
A single word can create an unbridgeable distance.
People become mortal enemies over a remark.
Old friends glow in hatred at one another.
Forgiveness impossible. Period.
With age words attain
an unhelpful weight. I'm finished with you!
Such brutal powerlessness.

The will to hurt, to kill.
As mysterious as self-hatred.

What we can't speak
we must be silent about.
But our eyes speak
straight through hatred
and loneliness.

I got lost in a strange part of town.
All streets ran steeply upward, quick-footed people
ran by me dressed in light-coloured clothes
and looking as though they were carrying light things in their bags.
I stopped someone for directions
and immediately I stood in the middle of a clump
of friendly faces. – Where do you want to go?
I began explaining. They listened,
smiling, as if for the first time
they were hearing a dead dialect.
Then they began speaking one on top of another
and pointing in all directions.
I pulled out my map. Eagerly it was opened
and studied with interest. – Where are we?
I asked with a finger on the map.
They looked at me and as a chorus repeated my question.
Then they all broke into hearty laughter,
I laughed too, we were witnessing high
comedy. – Here, said one of them and pointed
to the ground where we stood. – We are here!

Bitterness is the most durable result
of much human activity –
and you can't use it for anything,
so everyone denies it exists.
Most store it in the back room,
it is toxic with a nasty colour.

During busy times it plays dead
lying desiccated in its little box
but as soon as there's an unguarded moment
it demands attention. It lives off
injuries and thrives perfectly well in winter;
Christmas is a festival for it.

When bitterness is fully grown
it demands to be aired. Some
take it along to the pub on the weekend,
that works. Monday they show up at work
and begin again. Bitterness longs
for 5 p.m.; it speaks loudly to itself
in traffic and may hawk a gob.

Certain species prefer to live in exile.
There bitterness can run free.
It refuses to learn the language
and lives on a diet of fermented insults.
If it is rich, France is perfect.
Well cared for, bitterness can
grow to a good size.

Most important is to avoid mirrors
and emotional affiliations.

SAY SOMETHING

The one
who says nothing
imagines
the silence
that surrounds his silence
says everything.

But that silence
speaks in its own voice
that's the problem.

What's most important happens
in the silent zone
but no one can control that.
There angels and demons speak in chorus.

If you want something said
you'll have to say it yourself.

LODGE BROTHERS

The photo is on the front page
they are easy to identify, they move
comfortably in editorial offices. Honorary Doctorates,
they demand tributes
preferably torch processions. They squeeze out
dry little turds at jubilees.
Self-praise is usually genuine.

BY CHANCE

By chance in the morning traffic one meets
a person one hasn't spoken to
in more than twenty years; well, we've never actually
spoken but we've remembered
one another and followed each other's lives
at a distance without knowing details.
And still such a smile, a hello
and a quick handshake can illumine
the bicycle paths and send a warm wave of
happiness and gratitude through the body
against the spirits that govern the world.

Whenever I visited she had to be helped
to the toilet. Her brittle hips in a flabby
sack of skin. I lifted and supported
until she stood vibrating in her walker. Her chalk white
ancient hair turned like a low hanging moon;
she was no bigger than a ten-year old.

Her hands squeezed the handles of the walker,
with them she had peeled thousands of kilos
of potatoes and sewed her own dresses.
I could see her fingers turning over a penny
a long time ago, valuable and sparklingly new.
The same royal coin that later became void
just as inflation gobbled up everything she had toiled for.

90 years old, she had not given up
protesting. On the table lay Missionary Times
and yesterday's newspaper with its obituaries
which she investigated with a magnifying glass
in a stubborn attempt at finding a bannister.

The nursing home's toilet smelled strongly
of hospital. I loosened her leggings
and closed my eyes; supported my forehead against the tiles
and watched a strange movie: myself as dead,
my children shriveled and old some place in the future.
Just then she grabbed hold of me, commanding
me to return to now to help her up.

Step by step we worked our way back to the table
with the obituaries. I read them aloud for her
and she listened eagerly for well-known names
while she smiled inscrutably
as if she finally sat in a rain of pennies
soundlessly falling in her memories.

All religions are hypotheses
that God could probably do without.
    The snobs maintain
that life is totally
meaningless. Well, that's up to them.

That I am going to die was a matter of course
from day one. Everything around us
dies; some people live in apartments
festering with dead flies.

What matters is to face this
without resignation or becoming cynical.
    In the midst of living, surrounded
by children's spicy expectations.

The advantage of speaking a dialect is
that words are spoken and lived, before they are
thought and written. Dialects have no other
purpose than to handle the endless stream
of things and situations reality
is screwed together from.

All talk that isn't about real things
is actually nonsense. And pathetic nonsense
doesn't thrive well in a dialect.
All dialects have inbuilt nonsense detectors.
That's why very few people with political
ambitions speak with a dialect.

For the same reason it would probably be useful
to translate some new poems into dialect.
The ones that stand up to that treatment
are prob'ly not s'bad..

Of course even in dialect
it is possible to call a shovel
a spade or a spade a shovel.
But it wouldn't work for long.
Most people who speak a dialect
have held one in their hands.

The dream of going home
and walking in clogs forever.

No more running around lost and stressed out in an airport,
taking part in futile receptions,
wasting time in useless meetings.

Living with a blank calendar
at a respectful distance from everyone.

Standing at the gable and staring
after the migratory birds
in March and October,
content
not having to go anywhere.

Listening to the wind
going hunting for a while
comfortable with one's fear.

Seeing the sun rise and set
without problems,
pissing in peace
against one's own fence post.

Standing in one's clogs
and studying the stars
like a human being.

Is that too much
to demand of life?

He had begun to die.
I visited my father in the hospital,
he lay in a white bed which was clean and sinister.
    But he didn't want
to lie there, he wanted to get up again,
    get out of there.

He was on the sixth floor, with a view;
outside was a firestorm.
    Trees fell,
road signs banged on their hinges
Cars zigzagged below,
as if everyone was dead drunk.

But in here it was quiet,
    dead calm.
    My father's lips,
the sound of his hands against the duvet.
We touched each other.
He had almost used up all his words,
the ones he had left meant: out,
    home, off to work.

His innards were destroyed
from cancer; the doctors had opened him
and closed him again. Unbearable pain.
    He didn't say that.
He tried to fool the nurses,
    the doctor, himself.

He rang the bell, and they arrived.
        –   I have to get up.
He sat at the edge of the bed
his white legs and a swollen hand
dangling.

Two nurses laid his arms
across their shoulders to help him up.
Their knees trembled beneath the burden.
    Pain screamed through my father's
bones, he grew white around his mouth,
like a corpse. He wanted to get up.
    Stand.

Later, in bed, he breathed in pain.
I had to catch the train around midnight –
    walking about, smoking.
We could say anything
to each other now, but all words
were crippled. Goodbye he said.
    His eyes
said something more.

Everything collapsed. I walked to the train station
through empty streets, where the hurricane roared
    furiously,
tore at houses, trees, my clothes.
Debris slid across the asphalt,
as if the world was being torn apart,
    or was tearing itself loose now.

Inside me lives a windblown crofter,
his soul belongs on the heather. He doesn't trust
either God or the Devil.
He cooks his own stew and smashes
boulders with a heavy sledgehammer.
He is a heathen. He feels family
with wild animals. Seeing a human
gives him shivers all over his body.

He attends church on Sundays
to hear the organ. Inside
he roars in a deep bass, his soul steams
like boiling cement. Outside
he spits on the gravel. He wants to go home
to his own straw.
He walks among the windbreaks
to stand alone and piss against the wind.
He shakes off like a dog emerging
from a sewer.

DOUBLE EXPOSURE

You were in my thoughts
when I lay awake
unable to sleep.

Then I fell asleep,
and you were there, too.

A TERRIBLE HAPPINESS

Love is a terrible
happiness and misfortune
when it arrives with catastrophe
flashing lights and blaring sirens.
Traffic stops with anxious respect;
no one wants to be inside
that particular ambulance.

THE SOUL DANCES IN ITS CRADLE

If it is true that the soul
is born old
and grows younger throughout life,
then you and I are both older
and younger than one another.
That kind of fusion is dangerous.

Let's be honest: every day
we live with Fate
just like people who live in a delta
overrun by tides.
They are intimate with the moon;
we live on it.

The heart beats freely, the soul
dances in its cradle.

In the dialect I spoke as a child
we couldn't say 'my love,'
'I love you' or 'beautiful'.
We saw concepts like that as
expressions of hysteria;
besides, those words were too classy for us,
they didn't suit the work clothes
we wore. Much later I learned
that beauty is a reality,
and that feelings can be expressed directly in words.
But to see yourself as a victim
is only self-delusion. Certain words
still cause difficulty.

WHAT SHE HAS TWO OF

I.

Her two hands
are bewitched
    by preludes
to an unknown song;
she knows what it
    is going to be about,
that is the mystery.

It all succeeds
    in the moment,
heavy blood runs
into the fingertips.
But the mother of doubt
is always pregnant,
and every joy
is ravaged by anxiety
    and inner hurricanes,
that's how the piano plays!

After the catastrophe
magic seconds
arrive,
    the mind trembles
in euphoric fury,
her two hands
murder each other,
they fly about
    the whole house.
Then they do the dishes
and smash a plate,
then they attack the phone.

What is she playing?
It's probably Liszt.

2.

I prefer to get lost
    in your two eyes;
they are so real,
like two metaphysical
    novels,
each with its own plot.

Once I saw them
repeat an insane
    story.
Once I saw them attack
    like two predators.
Once I saw them
look out dreamily
    from a taxi.
Once I saw them
faint in joy
    at the sight
of two butterflies
flying over the abyss
and straight into the September
    sky.

Your eyes are two huge
    bonfires at the edge of the woods
where my stone age fears
set up camp, summer
    and winter.

Once I saw your eyes
open while you slept,
and it was a corner
of your soul I saw.

LOVE

It is such a big word.
Or did I choke on it?
Love, what is it
in the end?
Over time many exchange
big love for pennies.
I love you. And you tear out the plug.
I love you. And you fling my book
at the back of my head.
I love you. And the world explodes.

We thirst for each other in ignorance,
like elephants.

Without children no happiness,
said Schumann. Clara bore him
seven children as antidote against melancholia.
It wasn't enough.
He went insane, attempted suicide
and died in a sanatorium.
She played piano. That's what
they call love.

CAFE PUSHKIN

Now we live as if in a Russian novel
written in verse, by Aleksandr Pushkin.
We are the ones changing the street signs
but we are needy
and sleep in the same bed under a mountain
of clothes while the frost creaks.
Now Moscow is
again Moscow
and we trudge on. Everything is a lie
just as in reality.

You fantasize about stealing the machine gun
from a sleeping soldier,
but the soldiers stay awake
all night with you.
And you dance all night in Cafe Pushkin,
while I stand in the cloakroom
smoking Russian cigarettes,
what else?
Now you are called Natalia
and talk like someone who's crazy
crazy crazy.

And Pushkin was actually murdered
by her lover.

APHASIA

When you see a monkey banging a clam
against a stone it is like seeing one's self
     investigating a philosophical problem.
No one can preclude that animals are cleverer
than us, they manage life without words,
     we're unable to do that. Silence
leads us astray in a psychic labyrinth,
words flicker through the brain like fish
deep down; they constantly shift meaning.

Each of us finds our self in a body;
it is possible to make contact with caresses,
but everything becomes more and more abstract.
Foxes have holes and the birds of the sky have nests;
     the mind remembers the settlements
in raw nature. Now we live with bookcases
full of dictionaries, in nameless castles of air,
     on separate floors.
     What do you call that?

Why do you push each other so hard
in the bus, winter is dismal enough
    as it is.
What do we know of goodness
and of wickedness? Let us not contribute
to the smell of fear.
Most people take great care
    at living,
and anyone, who each morning undertakes
to get up, deserves respect.

During the killings unaware
we walked along the lakes.
You spoke of Szymanowski,
I studied a rook
picking at dog shit.
Each of us caught up in ourselves
surrounded by a shell of ignorance
that protects our prejudices.

The holists believe that a butterfly in the Himalayas
with the flap of a wing can influence the climate
in Antartica. It may be true.
But where the tanks roll in
and flesh and blood drip from the trees
that is no comfort.

Searching for truth is like hunting lizards
in the dark. The grapes are from South Africa,
the rice from Pakistan, the dates grown in Iran.
We support the idea of open borders
for fruit and vegetables,
but however we twist and turn
the ass is at the back.

The dead are buried deep inside the newspaper,
so that we, unaffected, can sit on a bench
on the outskirts of paradise
and dream of butterflies.

It happens that I am suddenly hit by, you know – it –
when we're watching the news with children in the room.
Their serious restlessness at the sight of murder
and the sound of crying condenses
into a big question mark hanging
above my head like an axe
or a dirty cloud.

I switch it off. I attempt to erase
it all, shift the mood. In vain.
Smashing the TV won't do it either.
The truth about the state of the world seeps
in through the walls; the children know,
of course, it's their world –
the only one I have for them.
You can see it in their eyes;
they will not acquit us. Never.
Our jokes are without effect,
cynicism builds minus points.
Each day ever more is piled up
of, you know – it.

Can the world be improved? First we'll have to change
human nature. There's cause for pessimism.
Evil triumphs and hate appears clothed
in religion, or in the latest political uniform.

But it is more difficult yet to give up on the idea
and to resign oneself to the world as it is. So we must
let go of the dream that our descendants will meet
a happier future. Genetic inheritance.

And none of us can imagine killing off our children's
expectations, even if we are ashamed of our own
confusion and ignorance. Joy is such a frail
material, and physical happiness is no crime.

Admitted; I'm groping in the dark. There's a shortage
of words with real validity. Concrete
suggestions or a solid sentence with a foothold.
I cannot offer firm arguments.

But I'm affiliated with the naïve who mosey on
and want the impossible.

The fools of the world blabber away
like a stupid door banging
in the wind. Everyone listens to it
because it is impossible to avoid;
its resentful ruckus drowns out
music and intimate conversations.
It prevents any reflection,
which is its only purpose;
complete nonsense. No one understands
its simplistic proclamations.
We eat our meals to the sound
of that idiotic door.
Its moronic din continues
all night; it seeps into sleep
and blends with our dreams.
Whenever you think it's over
it begins again. The door yells
and scolds itself with its own mouth.
That's how it is with fools.

AXIOM

False pride
   collapses
sooner or later.
As if reality
in its innermost
structure were governed
   by reason.

Despots and empires
grind to an end;
brutal murderers
and violent political
   systems
last for only a time,
then the regime falls
apart from
   the inside.

The dictator's name
disappears
into the great forgetting –
faster than the representatives
   of goodness
whom the heart remembers.

New incarnations
of human evil
   appear –
brutality and arrogance
mate happily
with our own desire
   for a jackpot.

But the new ones
and their servile
fellow-travelers
will also disappear

when
their time comes.
Trust that.

Invincible
   is the marrow
which every morning
lifts us all
out of sleep
   each with our own
flopping catch
of joy and hope.

ENCOURAGEMENT

Isn't it an uplifting thought
that in a few decades we
and this whole confused epoch
with its retarded presidents,
worn-out arguments,
mawkish TV hosts, dim journalists,
and the cepitalustic jubilant choir
will be gone?   For all time.
We will disappear.
They will disappear.
I will disappear.
You will disappear.
It will all disappear.
Hurrah!

Becoming a grownup. Politely greeting
confidential depressions,
yet still picking up one's tools
and getting things done, scrubbing
the toilet.

People travel around the globe.
You go to the baker's;
                read shopping lists
                others have lost –
                perhaps that's how
                He announces Himself.

Each day you wash the dishes.
Tomorrow they'll need doing again.

Alone at home with your stubborn
defeats. The heart startles.
Behind every word an illusion
laughs. Face God,
buddy.

My dead Father comes to visit
and sits down in his chair again, the one I got.
Well, Niels he says.
He is brown and strong, his hair shines like black lacquer.
Once he moved other people's gravestones around
using a steel rod and a wheelbarrow, I helped him.
Now he's moved his own
by himself. How's it going? he says.
I tell him all of it,
my plans, all the unsuccessful attempts.
On my bulletin board hang seventeen bills.
Throw them away,
he says, they'll come back again.
He laughs.
For many years I was hard on myself,
he says, I lay awake mulling
to become a decent person.
That's important.

I offer him a cigarette,
but he has stopped smoking now.
Outside the sun sets fire to the roofs and chimneys,
the garbagemen make noise and yell to each other
on the street. My Father gets up,
goes to the window and looks down at them.
They are busy, he says, that's good.
Do something!

PROBLEMS

Problems have a disagreeable tendency
to become personal,
they may well disturb one's perspective.
If you are certain of something
you can take for granted that you're wrong.
All the world's brutality is due to people
often considering themselves more clever, better
or wittier than others. An elementary error
most of us are caught in; everyone is a saint
in his own mythology. But the eternal truth
out of Hørsholm is merely a bad joke
in Herlev; and Ishøj has a totally different agenda.

The beauty of morning at the end of August,
Haydn on the radio.
Alone in the sparkling light
with the simple fact.

I ought to have done everything differently,
that's easy enough to see.
As a rule I was out of step,
preoccupied by the most trivial chores,
caught in banal worries about money
or feeling exalted by just being.
This is how I spent time,
                    my time on earth,
hunting for weekly bargains, repairing bicycles,
reading the newspaper, discussing politics, watching TV
and playing soccer. A fiasco
at all disciplines.

Often I neglected doing more useful things
in order to ponder the mystery,
in the hope of catching a thought
or the proper articulation in flight.

Was it myself I was at war with?
To look truth in the eyes
is just as unbearable as staring
into the sun. Real insanity
looks normal.

To write is an utterly futile
activity, it's true.
Words on paper make no difference
anywhere in the cosmos –
a book is just a book.
It's shelved in a bookcase
among millions of other books,
until it grows mould or rots
and is thrown away and burned
along with all sorts of garbage.

To write books is only one
of many ways of understanding one's life.
Those of us who scribble are all
in a competition of the handicapped,
some see themselves as
important, with no reasonable grounds.
Some level-headedness is called for.
The water truck driver who flushes
the city's sewers is more useful
than most of us;
give the GG to him.

In Naples I chanced upon Halldór Laxness. It was strange,
because he had died that spring. He smiled, delighted
beneath his newly-trimmed moustache and walked quickly through
the spacious room, an unostentatious restaurant
with white tableclothes near Piazza Garibaldi.

He seemed in good health, dressed in light pants
and a plaid tweed jacket, just like the photos
from Iceland in the fifties. He sat down at a table occupied
by a woman and a man, and the three of them spoke spiritedly
to each other in Italian, while the waiter served wine
and various courses for them; first pasta,
then fish, bread and salad.

Halldór Laxness ate with gusto,
his laughter braying, and he was engaged in the conversation.
That pleased me, I had heard he'd grown senile and,
besides, he was dead.

When their meal was almost over, I felt like
going over to say hello, tell him how glad I was
to see him hale and well. But I lacked the words,
and perhaps he wouldn't like being recognized
in a strange country, now that he was dead.
Instead I listened intensely to their conversation,
when suddenly I managed to catch an utterly
clear reply: 'The God of humans is of varying greatness,
just like they are,' Laxness said. 'Small people have small gods,
and the small-minded look in vain
for Him in a microscope.' He laughed heartily.

In the end the two Italians got up from the table.
The woman gave a little speech while she brought out a parcel
the size of a book and gave it to Halldór Laxness.
He opened the parcel with great care.
It turned out to contain a pair of socks, possibly silk.
Haldór Laxness was moved, tears welled in his eyes,

and he said something in a soft slurred voice. I couldn't
make out every word, but his Italian was beautiful,
and I understood him to say: 'Thank you,
that is a good gift. And it's not even
my birthday.'

THE TASK

To wake up at night with a brain filled with insane
speculations is not so special,
most people have to face a monster. Some have to
take meds to bear the pain,
to survive a loss or slip out of a depression.
They feel totally abandoned and alone
with the ogres – that's how it is.
The devil walks about like a roaring lion.

Others make do with whatever dope is on the market
in retail: tobacco, coffee, alcohol, orgies in food
or in asceticism. Some succeed in disappearing
into work, or some other splendid passion.
We build small empires in the hope that they'll serve
as fixtures for our homeless spirits on the day
we leave our bodies and step into eternity.

Everyone wants to leave their tracks – as a thank-you
that we were granted permission to step on the earth and enjoy
it's beauty; granted permission to love and hate
to the normal extent in a body with a normal address.

The task is for us to decipher our common experiences;
the horror and the misery that surround us, cling
to our clothes and seep into all of our bodies.
To notice what's going on, and if possible
to say things as they are.

THE MAGPIE

What a racket
in the backyard, damnit.
The magpie, that little hysteric

doesn't care that the poet
refuses to write
about such a silly bird:

Fuck you! Fuck you!

A LITTLE SELF-IRONY

                    A little
self-irony suits all
            the others
when the day empties its pockets,
and winter's churlish
            depressions
have an assignation on the stairs.

We spoke of heart problems
and sudden deaths;
jokes were told
of potato chips, wine and cigarettes.
We ate and drank. Our touch was light
because none of us doubted
that one day we too will find ourselves lying
each, alone, on the sidewalk or some floor
with a view of feet and chair legs,
while someone frantically tears
buttons from our clothes
and screams for help.

There's no shame
in dying on the floor,
as long as it's not
on purpose.

EPIGRAM

You can spend an entire life
in the company of words
not ever finding
the right one.

Just like a wretched fish
wrapped in Hungarian newspapers.
For one thing it is dead,
for another it doesn't understand
Hungarian.

NIELS HAV is a poet and short story writer living in Copenhagen with his wife, pianist Christina Bjørkøe. He has published five books of poetry and three collections of short fiction. An earlier English edition of Hav's work titled *God's Blue Morris* was published in Canada in 1992, and the team of Friesen and Brask were also the translators for this collection. Hav's work has appeared in other languages as well, including English, Spanish, Italian, Turkish, and Portuguese; a collection also appeared in Macedonian published by Spektar Press. Next year a collection will appear in Istanbul, Turkey. Hav has been the recipient of a number of prestigious awards. He has travelled widely in Europe, Asia, North and South America.

PATRICK FRIESEN is a poet, playwright, essayist and translator who lives in Vancouver. He has collaborated in the translation of three volumes of Danish poetry with P. K. Brask. Friesen teaches at Kwantlen University College.

P.K. BRASK is a translator of poetry, drama and short fiction who has collaborated with Patrick Friesen on three collections of Danish poetry. He is Professor of Theatre and Film at the University of Winnipeg.

ACKNOWLEDGEMENTS

The poems in this collection are all from *Grundstof* (Gyldendal 2004), except 'Cafe Pushkin', 'Women of Copenhagen', 'Visit from my Father', 'My Fantastic Pen', 'In Defence of Poets' and 'Epigram' which were first published in *Når jeg bliver blind* (Gyldendal 1995). 'A Mystery' is printed for the first time here.

Some of these poems have previously appeared in *EVENT, Danish Literary Magazine, Politiken, Information, God's Blue Morris, Linden Lane Magazine, POET, Victor B. Andersens Maskinfabrik, Vinduet, Horisont, Insancil* and *Literaturen Vestnik*.

Danish is a small language spoken by only 5 – 6 million people. To gain contact with the rest of the world translation is necessary. Patrick Friesen and P.K. Brask have been following my work for more than fifteen years. Their enthusiasm and support has been very healthy for my soul – and of invaluable importance to my work. I want to express my gratitude. The careful and inspired translations made by Patrick Friesen and P.K.Brask – both prominent in their work – has made it possible for my poems to travel around the Globe and across the Atlantic; now We Are Here.

Niels Hav

COLOPHON

Manufactured in an edition of 400 copies in the fall of 2006

English translation © Patrick Friesen and P.K. Brask
Original text copyright © Niels Hav & Gyldendal, Copenhagen 2004

First English Edition

Printed in Canada

Designed by Jay MillAr

BookThug : 33 Webb Avenue Toronto Ontario Canada M6P 1M4

Distributed by Apollinaire's Bookshoppe : www.bookthug.ca